KOKORO
MINDSTYLES
Guidebook

Kokoro MindStyles®

Kokoro MindStyle Guidebook

Companion Book for Kokoro MindStyle Cards

COACH TRAINING WORLD

Created by Feroshia R.J. Knight MA, MCC
Coach Training World (CTW)
www.coachtrainingworld.com
Portland, OR 97239, USA

Conquer Life's Challenges

How many times in your life have you experienced a challenging relationship? Whether it was personal or professional, you know the one — no matter what you do or say the issue remains (as do the recurring fights).

People may be willing to forgive, but they don't always forget. And when one pattern of reaction leads to another, you've got combustion on your hands. The fires that fuel our reactions can easily ignite us into a myriad of red hot problems that lead to damaged relationships and downright disasters in our relationships at home, work and play.

Maybe you've worked hard to improve your communication and approach. Or maybe you've fallen back to a place of personal safety and entered the mode of simply letting life "happen" to you. But no matter which approach you take, things don't improve and you end up feeling stuck.

What if you could release the defensive patterns of habit that lock you in a fight, flee or freeze response? And what if you could directly address challenging situations and move toward being able to connect with and relate to just about anyone — or at least remain unaffected by their presence — regardless of who they are or how they behave?

With over two decades of experience in effective Change Mastery, we are certain of one thing: the number one roadblock to success in mastering life's challenging moments is often the one person who has the power to change it… YOU!

Navigating the white waters of life is possible!

Change is the only constant in life. And our fear of the unknown is the only real inhibitor. It's what stops us from trying something new, keeping us locked in patterns far longer than desirable.

There are three courses of action based on our basic survival patterns: Fight, Flight and Freeze — all of which are fueled by FEAR. But what if there was another pathway — a middle road?

By acknowledging and bringing to heart our fears, we can safely and effectively release habitual reactions and inhibitions, instantly transitioning from resistance to flow while remaining centered, grounded and peaceful within.

As professional change makers, those of us at Coach Training World know the value of being able to see and shift in the moment. We've taught many life-long learners just like you how to smash life's challenges to smithereens once and for all.

And with the Kokoro: Life Mastery® system, that's exactly what we've created — an easy program of martial arts-like practices that enable you to live, work and play stress-free through a proactive approach, moving you away from simply fighting the daily "fires" of life toward what matters most.

Transition from surviving to thriving!

Kokoro — which translates to "from the heart" in Japanese — is the Martial Art of Life Mastery. It's centered in the belief that by unifying the energetic forces of mind, body, heart and spirit, we can defeat the challenges that hold us back while unleashing the momentum necessary to create whatever we desire most in our lives — especially when those desires are centered around a life full of happiness and enriched-living through rewarding relationships.

The Kokoro: Life Mastery® system stems from the theories and methodologies of Pattern Analysis, Positive Psychology, Emotional Intelligence, Somatic Coaching, Transformational Learning, Authentic Movement, Aikido, Tai Chi, Art Therapy and Systems Thinking.

Richly peppered with thought-provoking, experiential exercises, here are just a few of the topics that the KOKORO: Life Mastery workshops explore:

- Recognize & transform the survival dances that ensnare you in habitual, self-defeating patterns
- Shift reaction and misunderstanding into pro-action and collaboration

- Wield the sword of truth, hacking through complexity and uncertainty
- Transform conflict and inner turmoil through a process of actualization and accomplishment
- Climb to the top of the Life (Conflict) Mastery pyramid through truth, trust and transparency
- Effectively deploy the five Kokoro Keys to quickly identify the fastest steps and smartest shifts in how you think and behave in life
- Move toward peace, harmony and success in all that you think, feel, say and do
- Enjoy the benefits of being happy in all relationships, regardless of what life tosses your way

Similar to the study of any other martial art, Kokoro is centered on learning awareness. It's about being in the present, ready to face whatever's coming at you (a.k.a. - the reality of your situation) rather than what you imagine or fear.

The Kokoro system teaches you to leverage the forces around you, instead of allowing them to defeat or overwhelm you, and to remain balanced and in flow, effectively meeting whatever may jump into the path ahead.

A WORD OR TWO ON GENDER PRONOUNS...

The archetypes in this book use one of two gender pronouns. They are largely derived from the original Jungian elements that, he believed, form our collective unconscious. Yet as you'll quickly recognize in descriptions like Ruler (which receives a masculine pronoun) or Liberator (which is described using a feminine pronoun), each of these archetypes is easily interchangeable. In fact, Jung promoted the idea that we all possess some level of the opposite within us — a balance he termed anima and animus.

It's also important to acknowledge that the masculine and feminine are not the only two options available to us. Gender inclusive or preferred gender pronouns (PGPs) like "one," "ou," "zie," "sie," "ey," and "ve" are equally applicable and can be substituted within all of the archetypes in this book.

None of the archetypes to follow are intended to represent or define specific gender roles.

So which pronoun do you prefer?

Kokoro MindStyles

Accommodator
Achiever
Activist
Addict
Adventurer
Advocate
Artist
Blamer
Catalyst
Champion
Competitor
Controller
Coward
Creator
Deal Maker
Detective
Dominator
Dramatist
Educator
Engineer
Free Spirit
Fun Lover
Generalist

Healer
Hermit
Hero
Innocent
Intellectual
Jester
Joiner
Judge
Leader
Learner
Liberator
Lover
Loyalist
Maximizer
Mirror
Networker
Nurturer
Observer
Optimist
Outsider
Peacemaker
Princess
Protector

Provocateur
Questioner
Rain Maker
Realist
Risk Taker
Ruler
Saboteur
Sacrificer
Sage
Seducer
Servant
Shape Shifter
Spiritualist
Stabilizer
Star
Storyteller
Survivalist
Traditionalist
Vampire
Victim
Visionary
Warrior
Wizard

Table of Contents

To cultivate a successful experience by accounting for everyone's needs

ACCOMMODATOR

(Enabler, Pacifier, Yes Man)

Accommodator

Known as the one who makes room for others, the Accommodator is focused on ensuring a pleasant and successful experience for herself and others. She is highly adaptive and does everything within her power to ensure success for a team, project or relationship.

Sensitive to other people's emotions, especially uncomfortable ones, an Accommodator is known to keep the boat from rocking by perceiving the needs of others. She is often found alongside more dominant or needy personalities, or as a servant leader within a community or organization.

Resourceful Expressions
- Adapts quickly to meet the needs of others
- Thoughtful; prepares for situations in advance
- Intuits reactions and is prepared to mediate
- Cooperative, kind and inclusive; plays well with others
- Inquisitive; willing to act on behalf of others

Adaptations (Shadow)
- Placates others to avoid conflict or discomfort
- Trades honesty and authenticity for protection
- Risks own significance to maintain status or connection
- Undermines own self-worth in service to others

To accomplish and bring things to completion

ACHIEVER

(Accomplisher, Doer, Implementer)

Achiever

Known as the one who gets things done, the Achiever doesn't take no for an answer. With her keen intuitive understanding of the practical world, she is the expert at implementation, the one who enjoys overcoming obstacles to bring a project to completion.

The Achiever excels at taking the concrete steps necessary for transforming ideas into physical form. But don't get in her way with needless theorizing or analysis. Putting achievement above all other values, she willingly sacrifices relationships and goodwill to complete the task at hand.

Resourceful Expressions

- Goal-oriented; prefers action to analyzing, planning or overthinking
- Focused and driven, selfmotivated, energetic and enthusiastic
- Unstoppable; overcomes all obstacles
- Reliable; trusted to get the job done
- Competent & confident, seeks the resources needed to achieve

Adaptations (Shadow)

- Prone to impatience, impulsiveness, competitiveness
- Overachiever; can't say no; overcommits
- Prefers power over finesse
- Impulsive; acts often before agreements are reached
- Easily frustrated, especially by those who lack drive or the need for accomplishment

To stand and speak for those who cannot on their own

ACTIVIST

(Environmentalist, Lobbyist, Protestor)

Activist

Known as the one who stands on behalf of others, the Activist frequently supports people who are underrepresented or don't have a voice. Leveraging petitions, rallies and even legal action, she relentlessly and fearlessly defends those who cannot defend themselves. Though she's comfortable lobbying or working toward policy, her average day is spent within fields both rural and urban, working for the cause she is most passionate about. For this reason, she has also become increasingly tech-savvy, with social media serving as one of her most effective organizational tools.

Adventurous in nature, an activist is found on the front lines of socially-conscious, environmental or political movements, working to raise awareness and organize others.

Resourceful Expressions
- Stands by values
- Loyal to a cause; acts on it
- Unafraid to speak out
- Ignites action and positive momentum in others
- Motivates others into action

Adaptations (Shadow)
- Stubborn; agenda prevents acknowledgment of alternatives
- Inability to recognize how the "work" (a.k.a. cause) deprives Activist's family, friends and social connections
- Inability to relinquish causes, even when others move on
- Irrational and explosive; fights in ways that draw more attention to self than the cause
- Consumed by emotion

To serve as a role model for commitment and perseverance

ADDICT

(Glutton, Junkie, Work-a-holic)

Addict

Known as someone who is consumed by his latest or lasting obsession, the Addict labors under a pattern that repeats time and time again. Falling victim to classic substances like drugs, alcohol, caffeine, consumerism and sex, the Addict can also be ensnared by habits viewed by some as less harmful or even positive in certain circumstances, such as exercise, workaholism and adrenaline producing events.

But the Addict can also achieve great personal strides and encourage others to do the same. He uses his "low points" as a benchmark for future improvement. This feeling of accomplishment then segues into even greater developments in one or more areas of his life, greatly bolstering his confidence and can-do attitude.

Resourceful Expressions
- Self-disciplined and builds on success
- Develops great psychological strength and strong inner abilities when addiction is broken
- Serves as a valued mentor to others
- Humble; every day is better than the last

Adaptations (Shadow)
- Has to have "it," yet it's never enough
- Willing to compromise integrity, finances and personal relationships to maintain addiction
- Secretive; conceals actions and makes excuses when confronted
- Frequently confronted by feelings of shame and powerlessness in the absence of self-control
- Sometimes viewed as dishonest when focus of addiction becomes central to behavior

To explore where others have not gone

ADVENTURER
(Pioneer, Explorer, Trail Blazer)

Adventurer

Known as the trailblazer, the Adventurer fearlessly navigates in search of terrain where no one else has ventured. Terrain that takes him into spiritual, emotional and physical journeys where others often dare not travel. Whether he seeks a new method, spiritual awakening, novel idea or unseen place, he strikes out in a bold new direction and paves the way for others to follow in his footsteps.

Restless and unsatisfied with the status quo, a strong sense of curiosity and stubbornness in the face of obstacles greatly aid the Adventurer in his quest for a better way.

Resourceful Expressions
- Highly resourceful, practical and persistent
- Comfortable with the unknown; maps uncharted territory
- More willing to lead than to follow
- Confident; take the initiative to explore
- Undaunted by obstacles, problems or naysayers

Adaptations (Shadow)
- Highly individualistic; has trouble cooperating with others
- Prone to reinventing the wheel; resistant to "tried and true" methods
- Restless and impatient
- Overconfident even in the face of contrary evidence
- Unable to know when to stop or turn back

To advocate for an idea or project; to spread the news

ADVOCATE

(Broadcaster, Marketer, Messenger)

Advocate

Known as the enthusiastic one, the Advocate takes up an idea, cause, product, or bit of knowledge and spreads the word.

Naturally communicative and articulate, she enjoys both having access to information, as well as being its gatekeeper. The Advocate uses many different media to get her message across and to be the harbinger of good news.

Resourceful Expressions
- Extroverted, optimistic and enthusiastic; relates well with others
- Persuasive, infectious energy
- Skillful and confident communicator across different channels
- Knows how to re-purpose the message to various audiences
- Natural rapport and trust builder; finds commonalities between people
- Understands and empathizes with others

Adaptations (Shadow)
- Unable to maintain confidentiality; gossip
- Withholds or distorts information to serve selfish purposes
- Talks more than listens; overpowers others; says too much; speaks out of turn
- Assumes expertise when not earned
- Fervently believes her own proselytizing; overly subjective
- Shouts down or vilifies those with opposing views

To revel in self-expression and share it with the world

ARTIST

(Creative, Dancer, Painter, Musician)

Artist

Known as the creative one, the Artist synthesizes discreet sensory elements into wholeness and creates meaning through symbolic representation. The Artist archetype includes anyone who engages in visual, auditory, or kinesthetic disciplines in order to interpret what he sees, feels and experiences, recreating a unique form of expression in the process.

Imaginative, intuitive, exploratory, creative, expressive, focused and sensitive, the Artist possesses a finely tuned aesthetic appreciation and an ability to be in the flow, as he actively searches for beauty in the world.

Resourceful Expressions
- Strong right brain thinker; imaginative, intuitive, creative, expansive
- Visionary; sees what others do not
- Sensitive, innocent, impulsive, new
- Strong emotional expression and connection in work
- Innate sense of harmony, balance, beauty in all forms

Adaptations (Shadow)
- Lacks strong rational capacity
- Overly subjective
- Values the theoretical or imaginary over the practical
- Moody, temperamental, emotional, isolated
- Takes things personally
- Financially challenged; starving artist syndrome

To build a protective wall that shields from responsibility and blame

BLAMER

(Critic, Finger Pointer, Nay-Sayer)

Blamer

Known as someone who readily directs attention away from himself and toward someone or something else when things don't go his way. This highly defensive archetypal pattern usually appears when he feels insecure or is confronted by failure or similar uncomfortable emotions. A Blamer feels he's 'doing the best he can', often rejecting criticism — regardless of how constructive — as well as opportunities to develop and grow.

The Blamer builds a protective wall around himself, designed to conceal his perceived vulnerabilities and shortcomings. Everything is everyone else's fault. Dictatorial in nature, a Blamer must be obeyed lest you suffer his wrath.

Resourceful Expressions
- May respond productively to a list of options (i.e. "What do you think we should do?")
- Can be highly organized (but may also use this as a weapon against others)
- Unafraid to voice opinions

Adaptations (Shadow)
- Favorite saying: "It's not my fault."
- Takes no responsibility for personal actions
- Has extreme difficultly admitting wrongdoing; never apologizes
- Engages with an aggressive posture: leaning slightly forward, head somewhat down; uses gestures to punctuate communication
- Strong tendency to micromanage
- Dislikes change and may work to sabotage it, for self as well as others
- Tends to exaggerate personal problems as well as achievements

To ignite people, possibilities, projects and processes

CATALYST

(Activator, Energizer, Fire-Starter)

Catalyst

Known as the one who "gets the ball rolling," the Catalyst possesses an abundance of energy to initiate. While he is always the one willing to light the fire, to do whatever it takes to set things in motion, rarely does he sustain his furious drive through to the end of the project.

Known for his infectious energy and convincing nature, the Catalyst motivates others through feats of courage as he daringly jumps into the ring himself, convincing others to follow his lead.

Resourceful Expressions
- Energetic and enthusiastic; awakens others
- Intuitively understands first steps, where to start
- Understands how to motivate others; convinces through emotion
- Natural booster for ideas, products and projects

Adaptations (Shadow)
- Pushy and impatient
- Overwhelms those who aren't quite onboard with the idea or process
- Lacks follow-through; does not complete what he starts
- Leaves others to pick up the ball or assemble the pieces
- Impulsive; fails to think things through before acting; easily overwhelmed

To exude competence and confidence

CHAMPION

(Athlete, Numero Uno, Victor, Winner)

Champion

Known as the one who "goes the distance," the Champion is willing to sacrifice everything to reach her goal. With her eye ever on the prize, she works diligently, often toiling for little money or recognition. Possessing a strong inner drive, the Champion inspires others with her self-discipline and single-minded focus on the desired outcome.

She thrives on conquering new territories or never-before accomplishments. Continuously striving for higher goals, the Champion will compete against herself and her personal best if she lacks competitors in her class.

Resourceful Expressions
- Disciplined, focused, goal-oriented, self-sacrificing
- Puts ego concerns below the good of the cause
- Strength of will and character; mind over matter
- Uplifts others; inspires the best in others; role model
- Driven; highly focused, unstoppable

Adaptations (Shadow)
- Expects too much of self and others; self-destructive
- Struggles; incites conflict; pushy
- Lives only in the future
- Once on a path, has difficulty changing course
- Unrealistic about rewards
- Agressive; never good enough

To tirelessly strive past others and make it to "the top"

COMPETITOR
(Adversary, Opponent, Rival)

Competitor

Known as someone who is continuously striving to get to "the top." While the Competitor often possesses considerable expertise, she frequently uses it in service to her own advancement rather than that of others. Her primary goal is to be seen and celebrated as possessing more talents, experience or process knowledge than others, even when this level of recognition is unwarranted.

Believing she can overcome any obstacle, a Competitor may be competing against herself, others or a combination of both. She is the one who seeks to rise above "the herd" and enjoy the recognition that accompanies peak performance. Unfortunately, her competitive streak often finds her burning bridges to reach goals.

Resourceful Expressions
- Works hard and enjoys the spotlight
- Strong commitment to perseverance
- Fast learner; adept at studying, adopting and adapting the successes of others
- Self-confident with a winning, "can-do" attitude
- Constantly seeks to improve; wants to be better than the day, month or year before

Adaptations (Shadow)
- Tendency to act unfairly and use passive aggressive behavior
- Focused on numbers rather than quality; prefers a large adoring audience to a few well-chosen confidants or colleagues
- Frequently feels overlooked or undervalued
- Would rather build new than develop existing
- Perceived as arrogant or conceited
- Views a loss as defeat
- May suffer from certain forms of anxiety

To oversee people, processes, projects

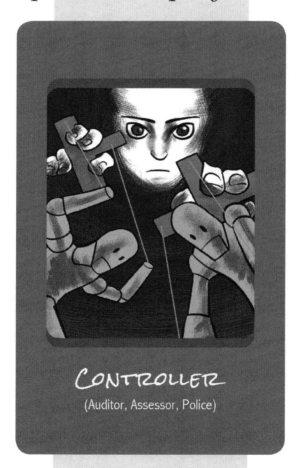

CONTROLLER

(Auditor, Assessor, Police)

Controller

Known as the person in charge, the Controller is the individual others observe to be the final decision maker about actions affecting the future of a group of people, a project or a process. Often because of his natural leadership abilities, others charge him with safeguarding the agreed-upon goals, visions or intentions while delegating the necessary tasks of the group.

Accountable and able to accept a great deal of responsibility, the Controller is the charismatic generalist who always keeps his eye on the details.

Resourceful Expressions
- Flexible, adaptable, adept at delegating tasks
- Has the good of the organization in mind
- Charismatic personality; trustworthy, likeable, influential
- Cuts through the noise to focus on what matters; decisive
- Process oriented, organized project manager

Adaptations (Shadow)
- Manipulative, coercive, demanding, abrasive, condescending
- Selfish; fails to take others opinions and needs into account
- Autocratic, egotistical
- Brutal toward those who are weak or dissenting
- Disconnected from the feelings and needs of others

To overcome fear and model bravery for others

COWARD

(Avoider, Chicken, Escapist, Retreater)

Coward

Known as the "spineless one," the Coward avoids danger and risk, especially through bravado, false-confidence and aggressive behavior. In a constant duel with fear, the Coward, often attracts bullies. Although he can be quite aggressively emotional in a fight, he prefers to turn tail rather than to put up a fight.

Even still, the Coward runs most swiftly from his own internal threats. In so doing, he points out to others the importance of overcoming personal obstacles.

Resourceful Expressions
- Reminds others to check their fears
- Tender-hearted; sensitive
- Self-knowledgeable; honest
- Self-preserving, survivalist

Adaptations (Shadow)
- Drops the ball when things get tough
- Betrays others
- Puts up a false front; behaves bravely but lacks follow-through
- Untrusting and risk-averse; unwilling to take even healthy risks

To identify and build what others can't even imagine

CREATOR

(Innovator, Inventor, Originator)

Creator

Known as someone who innovates, the Creator imagines, designs and often builds or fashions something with her own hands. The Creator places great trust in the creative process because she is confident in her ability to see it through. Closely related to the Visionary, a Creator takes a project from its conception to completion. Whatever she creates usually features a perfect balance of practicality and beauty.

Traditionally, the Creator is viewed as a god figure. But within this archetype, she is responsible for creating something new and often better. These creations can range from a software platform or an eco-friendly building to a recipe that incorporates ingredients in an innovative or unexpected yet pleasing way. Quite rare, true Creators reportedly account for less than 1% of the population.

Resourceful Expressions
- Unlimited well of imagination
- Ingenuity is an innate strength
- Comfortable with presentation and/or performance
- Seen as someone with "taste," who naturally finds harmony in words, musical notes, architectural angles, or other raw components and combines them effectively
- Likes to accomplish tasks

Adaptations (Shadow)
- Perfectionist tendencies
- Can become mired in frustration when things don't come together as expected
- Prefers hands-on contact with project, so may have trouble delegating or relinquishing control
- Project focus may detract from social skills, prohibiting effective communication and persuasion

To broker goods, services, or energy

DEAL MAKER
(Broker, Negotiator, Trader)

Deal Maker

Known as the wheeler-dealer, the Deal Maker knows what he wants and knows how to get it. Whether he's dealing with money, goods and services, or engaging in power plays, the Deal Maker is comfortable seeing life as a market-place in which to barter.

With a combination of charm and shrewdness, he greases the wheels in every type of human group, approaching all his relationships as a skilled negotiator.

Resourceful Expressions
- Shrewd, strategic, analytical
- Excellent negotiating skills
- Knows the value of things, people, skills and power
- Intuitively understands human nature; quick connector and trust-builder
- Seeks win-win for everyone

Adaptations (Shadow)
- Treats others like objects
- Sees every interaction as a transaction
- Manipulates knowledge and information to achieve desired outcome
- Lapses into "end justifies means" mentality

To discover the clues to uncover the truth

Detective
(Inspector, Investigator, Sleuth)

Detective

Known as the one who is hot on the trail, the Detective is the clue seeker in the group. He is never content to take information at face value, always striving to find underlying causes and to uncover the hidden properties of things, processes and even people.

The Detective's keen analytical mind easily forms hypotheses which he then tests by asking questions. Looking to the past he uncovers what is hidden in the present.

Resourceful Expressions
- Highly inquisitive; relentless searcher; ravenous for knowledge
- Analytical, theoretical and hypothetical thinker; objective
- Excellent communicator and listener
- Sees multiple paths and possibilities
- Strong intuitive sense; trusts hunches
- Uncovers the hidden or mysterious, including human motives

Adaptations (Shadow)
- Suspicious; doubts all that he can't validate; fearful
- Abrupt, pushy and unfeeling when seeking information from others
- Historically oriented; does not relate well to the future
- Obsessive; loses perspective when in search mode

To get things done, no matter the collateral damage

DOMINATOR

(Bully, Coward, Tyrant)

Dominator

KKnown as someone who often looks down on others, the Dominator archetype asserts his control whenever possible and may resort to assault (verbal or otherwise) to achieve that end. This archetype can be viewed as a protective pattern, preserving his feelings of individual safety by creating distance from others.

A Dominator is also frequently knowledgeable and kind-hearted. He can expound, often at great length, on his subject-matter expertise. Unfortunately, this is just as often coupled with a disinclination toward social cooperation due to a communication style that can be seen as loud and domineering. A Dominator issues demands, expects them to be followed immediately, and does not tolerate excuses.

Resourceful Expressions
- Thinks quickly and communicates in the same rapid-fire manner
- Assertive and focused on the immediate goal
- Open and direct
- Decisive and prefers to move quickly from one issue to the next

Adaptations (Shadow)
- Can view people as possessions that contribute to personal security/safety
- Rarely comfortable within social situations when not in control
- Often tolerates only those viewpoints and opinions that coincide with their own
- Fantasizes what a relationship should look like and entail
- Possessive

To model self-expression and communicate emotionally

DRAMATIST
(Actor, Actress, Drama Queen)

Dramatist

Known as the prima donna, the Drama Queen seizes every opportunity to openly express her feelings. She is not shy about her own needs and desires, and often attracts a great deal of attention to get them met.

Known for her elaborate, sometimes confusing behaviors, there is rarely a dull moment as the Drama Queen adapts her presentation to achieve the desired effect with her audience.

Resourceful Expressions
- Highly creatively expressive; eloquent
- Intuitive and right-brained; deeply emotional
- Tuned-in to the unexpressed energy in the situation
- Unafraid of confrontation or promotion of self, group, and ideas
- Energetic, lively; draws others out
- Freely expresses emotions; models free expression for others

Adaptations (Shadow)
- Distracting, disruptive; speaks and acts inappropriately
- Self-absorbed; attention-seeker; blind to others' needs and points of view
- High maintenance, uncooperative and difficult to please
- Uses drama to hide perceived inadequacies and deflect criticism
- Depressed, distressed and self-destructive

To bestow knowledge upon the next generation

EDUCATOR

(Lecturer, Professor, Teacher)

Educator

Known as a "disseminator of information," the Educator is an avid listener, learner and synthesizer of subject matter. He accumulates knowledge from personal experience and academic sources then translates it so others can reap the benefits of his scholarly devotion.

An Educator often serves as a teacher, professor, business mentor or trainer in a particular skill set or specialized body of knowledge. Often possessing elevated expectations, he teaches the next generation, promoting a sense of community and belonging through genuine enthusiasm and care. In some cultures, he also frequently doubles as the tribal- or family-elder. Other common examples include Zen masters, philosophers, priests and spiritual leaders.

Resourceful Expressions
- Curious; avid learner who is receptive to feedback
- Kind, compassionate and capable of fully engaging others
- Adaptive, flexible and recognizes what students need to thrive
- Devoted to sharing and continuously learning in the process
- Emotionally- and socially-intelligent
- Easily determines useful information
- Conscious as to delivery method; shifts to ensure learner is receiving the value needed

Adaptations (Shadow)
- Educates others as a way to gain influence, power and status
- Disregards thoughts out of alignment with own
- May teach undesirable traits, dishonest practices
- Unobservant of the true needs of others; talks "at" people
- Rigid and unable to accept challenges to own ideas
- Ineffective at organization

To organize, plan and strategize ideas

ENGINEER
(Analyst, Architext, Planner, Strategist)

Engineer

Known as the architect of information, the Engineer epitomizes left-brain problem solving by synthesizing information and systematically thinking through the obstacles.

For the Engineer, implementation is secondary to strategizing, planning and manipulating the necessary data to rationally address both practical and theoretical problems. He tends to objectively evaluate, and measure rather than to rely on intuition or gut response.

Resourceful Expressions
- Focused; not easily distracted
- Linear; exhibits a step-by-step thinking style
- Curious about how things work
- Highly independent and objective
- Analytic; reduces complex ideas and forms into component parts
- Resourceful; adept at finding the right process or tool to implement a design

Adaptations (Shadow)
- Unable to observe or understand context; reductionist
- Lacks trust in feelings, intuition and non-rational thinking styles
- Clumsy, forgetful, absent minded; checked-out
- Poor communication; difficulty with layman's terms
- Challenged when working on a team; excessively introverted

To enjoy and model personal independence

Free Spirit

(Individualist, Maverick, Non-Conformist)

Free Spirit

Known as the one who does her own thing, the Free Spirit is most often identified by a complete refusal to conform to social and group norms. Loathed or admired, Free Spirits attract attention for their unusual or eccentric behaviors and appearance.

Often these individualistic types, quite happy on their own, inspire others to take healthy risks, to free themselves from the shackles of peer and social pressures, and to live more authentically.

Resourceful Expressions
- Able to go it their own way; internally referenced; self-secure
- Work without much support or acknowledgment
- Out-of-the-box thinker
- Unafraid to take a stand, defend personal beliefs and rights
- Highly attuned to free will and spontaneity; trust in the journey

Adaptations (Shadow)
- Inconsiderate of others' agendas and opinions
- Difficulty forming close relationships; avoid commitment, responsibility
- Trouble cooperating in group situations
- Easily misunderstood by others; fear-provoking
- Willful, aggressive, disruptive
- Aloof, elsewhere, non-present; unstable and untrustworthy

To live in the moment and revel life's pleasures

FUN LOVER
(Bon Vivant, Hedonist, Indulger)

Fun Lover

Known as the life of the party, the Fun Lover lives fully in present time. Neither worried about the future nor regretting the past, the Fun Lover appears to joyfully enjoy every activity and sensual experience.

She invites others to join her as she does whatever she does for the sheer pleasure it brings, rewarding those lucky enough to follow her path with laughter, merriment and relaxation.

Resourceful Expressions
- Focuses on the physical experience; fully engages in joy and fun
- Fun to be with, enthusiastic, playful; gets along easily with others
- Lives out loud and invites others to do the same
- Sees the positive side of situations; able to make light of difficulties
- Great palate and eye for the creative arts
- Appreciates and cultivates the new and diverse

Adaptations (Shadow)
- Short-sighted and impractical
- Difficult to engage in serious endeavors; irreverent
- Dishonest; lives in fantasy world
- Reluctant to use rational mind
- Lacks steadiness and consistency
- Avoids discomfort, conflict and challenges
- Escapist; plays excessively to avoid the harder truths of life

To explore, experience, learn a myriad of things

GENERALIST
(Dabbler, Hobbyist, Jack-of-all-Trades)

Generalist

Known as the jack-of-all-trades, the Generalist is the person who passionately engages in their interests without the need to be the expert or professional. Driven by his interest in learning new things, the Generalist sometimes amasses an impressive body of knowledge in a specialized field or displays extraordinary skill at an esoteric art, simply out of sheer delight in pursuing his subject matter.

More typically, the Generalist prefers serial dabbling in just about anything new he can learn or try.

Resourceful Expressions
- Individualistic, independent, spontaneous, free
- Not limited by professional standards, proscribed methods or best practices
- Open, curious, inquisitive; passionate learner
- Values the novel; willing to try new things, contexts, ideas

Adaptations (Shadow)
- Difficult to pin down; flighty; inconsistent
- Doesn't know what he doesn't know
- Lacks focus to produce mastery; lacks devotion and follow-through
- Feels restricted when it's time to make a choice
- Avoids responsibility; doesn't "own" what he knows

To provide care and healing for others

HEALER
(Docter, Medicine Man, Therapist)

Healer

Known as the empathic one, the Healer diagnoses and cures the physical, emotional, mental and spiritual problems of others. The Healer brings compassion, skillful means and a true consideration for the health and well being of others, to her work, no matter her professional affiliation.

Not necessarily medically trained, but always motivated by the desire to serve others, the Healer often cures merely by her presence.

Resourceful Expressions

- Service oriented; focused on others
- Compassionate; intends to reduce suffering
- Superb diagnostic skills and intuitive understanding
- Engenders trust and respect in others; authentically connective
- Hands-on; solution oriented
- Respects others for who they are; unconditionally loving

Adaptations (Shadow)

- Uses healing power to manipulate others
- Fails to say what she sees
- Quackery; malpractice
- Motivated by power or greed
- Plays god; ego-centered
- Heals others while neglectful of self

To seek contemplative solitude

HERMIT
(Introvert, Loner, Monk, Recluse)

Hermit

Known as the quiet type, the Hermit is happiest alone in his cave. Others identify him more by his absence than by his presence, and consider him hard to get to know, secretive or just plain shy. The Hermit rarely says much, but when he does speak, a wealth of clear knowledge and understanding rings forth, borne of deep listening.

To others the quiet Hermit appears to be lying dormant, when in reality his mind is actively engaged in silent observation and immersion in a rich inner world.

Resourceful Expressions
- Solitude elicits unique insights and wisdom
- Deep listener, observer, thinker
- Vivid imaginative capacity
- Able to deeply absorb, digest and understand issues and situations
- Thinks before speaking; carefully considers impact of words
- Calm, steady and reassuring presence

Adaptations (Shadow)
- Trouble showing up, passive aggressive; refuses to engage
- Overwhelmed by the needs, energies and desires of others; fears overextending himself
- Doesn't speak-up when he could
- Hesitates, stalls, obfuscates for no reason
- Fearful, anxious, shy in groups
- Selfish with knowledge or sharing his gifts with the world; hoards energy and information

To exhibit bravery; to risk oneself on behalf of others

Hero
(Heroine, Protagonist, Rescuer)

Hero

Known as the one who saves the day, the Hero fights for good and rises above evil. Often seen as a larger-than-life figure, the Hero employs his special talent or gift to solve seemingly unsolvable problems or risky situations.

Always ready to face serious danger or death in order to prevent harm, the Hero stands tall as someone others look up to and admire.

Resourceful Expressions
- Motivated to rescue and serve
- Faces fear and obstacles head-on
- Emotionally intelligent; heart-centered
- Stays aligned with his values and the values of his community
- Confronts the status quo
- Steps up to do what others fear

Adaptations (Shadow)
- Grand-stands; egocentric; fears losing status or privileges
- Cowardly; bullies others to hide fear and impotence
- Reckless; puts self and others at risk
- Abuses power or status
- Competitive and impulsive; pushes when to do so will cause more harm than good

To engender purity, newness, possibility and play

INNOCENT
(Blank Slate, Child, Youth)

Innocent

Known as the naïve one, the Innocent is the person others see as pure, lacking guile or manipulation. The Innocent approaches every situation and person as if for the first time, bringing a freshness and playfulness to each encounter.

Completely in the moment, the Innocent helps others drop their preconceived ideas in order to engage in the creative process.

Resourceful Expressions
- Uninhibited, unconcerned about his image; egoless
- New, open, creative, curious; holistic and integrated thinker
- Playful; brings playfulness into relationships
- Accepts others unconditionally
- Imaginative; finds joy in the simple things

Adaptations (Shadow)
- Immature, untested, irrational
- Self-centered; solipsistic
- Unempowered; weak and helpless; needy
- Lacks discrimination and healthy boundaries
- Impulsive; easily flies off the handle; lacks self control
- Vulnerable to manipulation and control by others

To use rational intelligence to view the world

INTELLECTUAL
(Brain, Nerd, Philosopher, Thinker)

Intellectual

Known as the smart one, others see the Intellectual as confident in his ability to apply his rational thinking to problems, issues and ideas. They experience him as lost in thought. Indeed, the Intellectual rarely presents as a "people person," unless he entices a like-minded soul into a detailed debate about philosophy, politics or the history of ideas.

More often preferring the company of his books, charts and computer, the Intellectual enjoys the quiet solitude of his own mind.

Resourceful Expressions
- Left-brain dominant; highly analytical; theoretical
- Focused, determined, reclusive
- Quick-thinking; switches easily between details and the big picture
- Mentally creative and innovative; problem solver
- Uninhibited about expressing new or unusual thoughts
- Generalist; enjoys exploring varied topics and problems

Adaptations (Shadow)
- Clumsy; out-of-body; awkward
- Relates poorly with people and their emotions
- Ineffective communicator; unable to slow thoughts to speak coherently
- Nervous, neurotic, over-stimulated
- Over-processes; Unable to produce or finish things
- Challenged by emotional or dramatic people
- Cynical; all-knowing; know-it-all

To bring lightness, levity and joy to others

JESTER

(Comedian, Fool, Humorist, Joker)

Jester

Known as the class clown, the Jester brandishes the gift of making others laugh. Whether funny himself or merely blessed with a sense of wit and timing, the Jester lies in wait for the exactly appropriate (or inappropriate) moment to catch others off guard.

Always beguiling, with sensitive radar tuned to shifts in energy and mood, he lives in the moment, ever ready to take the seriousness level down a few notches.

Resourceful Expressions
- Sensitive and intuitive
- Great sense of energy, rhythm and timing
- Quick witted; spontaneous
- Able to diffuse tense situations
- Popular and easy to get along with; a people person
- Illuminates through humor and levity

Adaptations (Shadow)
- Jokes mask authentic feelings and truth
- Incapable taking anything seriously
- Escapist; lives in denial and fantasy
- Lacks ability to empathize with others; lonely
- Uses humor to wound; ambushes others
- Refuses to grow up; avoids serious or heated matters

To connect and fit in with others

JOINER

(Follower, Citizen, Member)

Joiner

Known as the organization's most committed member, the Joiner's drive for connection and belonging often finds them party to numerous clubs, committees and social groups. A Joiner is one who derives personal value from sharing her experiences in life with others. Whether it's a company soccer team or political group working toward the election of a specific cause or individual, the Joiner is usually the first one to arrive and the last to leave.

In the modern world, a Joiner can and does share her experience with the world via social media. Updates issue forth through a timeline that seems to be on a continuous scroll. As this level of involvement is required for her self-esteem, and the time required for many activities is often considerable, a Joiner can view herself as a step or two above others. She may also be easily swayed by the views of the organizations in which she participates. This makes her extremely susceptible to groupthink.

Resourceful Expressions
- Collaborative; interested in helping others
- Follower; highly supportive team member
- Easy-going; willing to go along with others
- Resourceful

Adaptations (Shadow)
- Self-righteousness
- Unwilling to take a stance that differs from the group
- Worries incessantly whether they "belong" in the group
- Takes the words and actions of others deeply personal

To arbitrate disputes, dispense justice and preserve equality

JUDGE

(Decider, Evaluator, Examiner)

Judge

Known as the one who decides, the Judge is the person everyone turns to when a verdict must be obtained. With his innate sense of right and wrong, the Judge willingly bears the responsibility for the entire group, ensuring objectivity and fairness for all.

Often serious and introspective, even as a young person the Judge has a bearing of maturity and thoughtfulness that naturally commands respect.

Resourceful Expressions
- Balanced right and left brain; easily synthesizes ideas and facts
- Mature and thoughtful bearing; commands respect
- Confident decision maker
- Gifted and direct, neutral communicator
- Able to remain objective, even-handed, rational and calm
- Holds sense of responsibility for ensuring the greater good
- Metes out justice fairly and without prejudice

Adaptations (Shadow)
- Judgmental and preachy
- Unable to relate to others in a down-to-earth way
- Overbearing, controlling and egoistic
- Hurts others with harsh words
- Masks authentic emotions with rational demeanor
- Plays favorites; biased

To motivate and support others to a future outcome

LEADER
(Commander, Inspirer, Motivator)

Leader

Known as the one who "leads the charge," the Leader guides others using his natural magnetism and communication skills. He never enters a room without becoming the center of energy; his charisma alone enables him to martial support while delegating the more menial tasks that make or break the endeavor.

A true Leader skillfully empowers others, furthering the agenda of the entire group in the process.

Resourceful Expressions
- Charismatic, magnetic, attractive
- Broad, big-picture thinker, visionary
- Superb communication skills
- Decisive, influential, practical, strategic
- Takes responsibility for failure as well as success
- Vulnerable and self-aware; honest with emotions

Adaptations (Shadow)
- Leads others astray with bad intention; victimizes others
- Egotistical, controlling, megalomaniacal
- Persuasive; manipulative
- Weak; panders to others
- Blames others for loss and failure
- Cowardly; fearful when under conflict

To seek knowledge and wisdom

LEARNER

(Apprentice, Seeker, Student)

Learner

Known as the "professional student," the Learner seems to have an insatiable curiosity. Preferring to "take in" rather than "put out," the Learner is often willing to go to great lengths to follow a lead, satisfy a hunch or sit at the feet of the wise elders of the community.

Young at heart, the Learner experiences the world as a never-ending and far-reaching school of life.

Resourceful Expressions
- Curious, inquisitive, great appetite for learning
- Goal-oriented and persistent
- Open; models listening for others
- Respects knowledge, wisdom and the traditions
- Naturally egoless; an empty cup waiting to be filled
- Becomes a repository of knowledge and asset to other seekers

Adaptations (Shadow)
- Always preparing rather than living life
- Refuses to grow up; eschews responsibility; refuses to own amassed knowledge
- Know it all; unsolicited advice-giver
- Teacher's pet; seeks attention for acquiring knowledge
- Hoards knowledge and information; selfish
- Lacks experience; lives life vicariously

To lead others toward personal freedom

LIBERATOR

(Emancipator, Luminary)

Liberator

Known as the one who lights the way, the Liberator is a natural freedom-seeker. She challenges others to confront their outdated beliefs. Rarely subtle, a Liberator breaks through the chaos and untethers the souls of others. She is driven by her own soul's calling and a belief in a world where everyone lives freely and authentically. Related to the Leader, this luminary leads toward freedom of mind, spirit and heart.

This archetype was traditionally reserved for great leaders, as well as those who freed people from oppression and other forms of mass tyranny. Examples include Martin Luther King, Jr., Nelson Mandela, Rosa Parks, Abraham Lincoln and Joan of Arc. Yet in today's world, the Liberator works tirelessly to release individuals from subjugation that is far subtler yet no less consuming. Modern Liberators address issues such as dietary habits, work-life imbalances, addiction and more!

Resourceful Expressions
- Sees the deeper potential of others
- Models freedom, peace and ease for the world around them
- Negotiates on behalf of others; uses logic and creativity to achieve desired results
- Well-equipped with numerous tools to help others break free
- Adept at working with the whole person

Adaptations (Shadow)
- Singular vision of how freedom looks; lost in own ideals
- Hermit; hides when doesn't know how to break others free
- Impatient; resists or becomes annoyed by those who prefer a more traditional or "safe" approach to life
- Uses angry, harsh words or other combative techniques to motivate others

To incite passion in relationships and endeavors

LOVER

(Appreciator, Romancer)

Lover

Known as the passionate one, the Lover fully engages her many heart-felt emotions while interacting with both people and things. The Lover easily includes others in her web of love, accepting and encouraging full expression of authentic and spontaneous feeling.

She is the group member who raises spirits when people become insecure or discouraged, bringing her warmth into every endeavor and eliciting passion in others.

Resourceful Expressions
- Generous with emotions; empathic and emotionally intelligent
- Easily expresses feelings and needs
- Sensual; playful and intimate
- Expert in verbal as well as non-verbal communication
- Inclusive; envelopes others in her passion
- Heart centered; unconditionally loving

Adaptations (Shadow)
- Prone to overly dramatic behavior
- Dislikes logical thinking; lost in fantasy; delusional
- Takes advantage of others' vulnerabilities
- Fickle; relies on vagaries of emotions
- Addicted to romantic encounters and inappropriate partners
- Reckless with emotions; victimized when rejected

To stand by a person, cause or organization

LOYALIST

(Ally, Companion, Devotee, Patriot)

Loyalist

Known as the best friend, the Loyalist often exhibits single-focused devotion to a cause, idea, person or group. If it's a political stand, she is prepared to take up arms if necessary. If it's personal in nature, she may become deeply protective of others.

Motivated by pure devotion and strong faith, the Loyalist is the companion or spouse who stays in a liaison through many trials, long after others would have moved on.

Resourceful Expressions
- Passionate, devoted, committed
- Strong value system; sees the good in the cause
- Single-minded, steadfast, unwavering, faithful
- Trustworthy; engenders belief and respect
- Puts others or the cause before his own self-interest

Adaptations (Shadow)
- Stubborn and irrational in the face of criticism
- Unable or unwilling to give up a "lost cause"
- Enables others; mistakes loyalty for belonging
- Rationalizes immoral or unjust behavior to further a cause
- Lacks self-esteem; relies on others for worth
- Lives vicariously through others

To help others step beyond their self-imposed limits

MAXIMIZER
(Coach, Developer, Facilitator)

Maximizer

Known as the "strength finder," the Maximizer takes pride in developing people, processes and systems, thereby activating and their highest potential. He is the one others count on to listen attentively and inspire new actions.

The Maximizer is able to map other people's thinking and behaviors. He then skillfully presents information to encourage change, including new perspectives, strategies and actions that enhance performance.

Resourceful Expressions
- Honest, open and effective communicator
- Easily builds trust and rapport with others
- Able to interpret people's thoughts and translate them to actions
- Adept at improving systems and processes
- Compassionate and helpful toward others
- Reflective, intuitive; guides from her own understanding and experience

Adaptations (Shadow)
- Uses rapport to manipulate and influence
- Maximizes personal and group power to meet her own agenda
- Directive, commanding; overly attached to particular outcomes
- Needy and attention-seeking
- Fixes processes and people that aren't broken
- Views self worth through others' eyes

To accurately reflect the true nature of other people

MIRROR

(Authentic Self, Truth Teller)

Mirror

Known as the truth teller, the Mirror speaks the truth often when others won't. Regardless of any discomfort, the Mirror authentically reflects information such that others can see themselves more clearly to create and deepen self-awareness in others.

Often confused with her cousin the Chameleon, the Mirror is unattached to her own identity or persona and thus freely reflects the thinking, actions and energy of everyone she encounters.

Resourceful Expressions
- Honest, open, direct and clear communicator
- Neutral observer
- Passive; receptive
- Lacks agenda
- Dispassionate; emotionless

Adaptations (Shadow)
- Induces fear in those unaccustomed to truth
- Magnifies faults or gifts
- Lacks interpretive faculty
- Cold; unfeeling

To connect people and resources to each other

NETWORKER

(Connector, Matchmaker, Socialite)

Networker

Known as the "mover and shaker," the Networker seems to know everyone and everything. Information is the currency with which he buys and brokers ideas, invitations and personal contacts.

Extroverted in nature, the Networker adroitly connects people and resources in his vast network, often through his intuitive understanding of human nature and society.

Resourceful Expressions
- Natural sales person; strong communicator
- Intuitively understands human nature
- Associative thinker; connective; sees links that others might miss
- Energetic, positive, enthusiastic team player
- Highly motivated to help others

Adaptations (Shadow)
- Prone to gossip; untrustworthy with confidential information
- Uses personal connections for selfish ends; name-dropper
- Lacks focus; easily distracted
- Talks more than listens
- Superficial; lacks depth of thinking and
- Noncommittal, especially to values, people or ideas

To nourish and care for others

Nurturer
(Adopter, Care Giver, Mother)

Nurturer

Known as the mothering type, the Nurturer takes good care of those around her. Soft and gentle or strict and disciplinarian, the good mother instinctively knows what is best for her underlings and she dispenses her wisdom and love accordingly.

Anyone, young or old, female or male, who loves and cares for others, can fulfill this role in a human group.

Resourceful Expressions

- Instinctive; emotional intelligence valued above intellect
- Heart-centered; instills comfort, ease, and a sense of being home
- Creative, life-giving, materially productive, fertile
- Strongly defensive of those under her care
- Reliably attentive to needs of others; trustworthy

Adaptations (Shadow)

- Ignores self-care; loses self in relationship to other
- Pushy, controlling, smothering, clinging, unhealthy attachments
- Enables others; infantilizes rather than aids growth
- Passive-aggressively withholds love and creative power
- Abuses her stature and power to further her own agenda
- Lives vicariously through those under her care

To witness others and be in the present moment

OBSERVER
(Bystander, Spectator, Watcher)

Observer

Known as the one looking in from a afar, the Observer takes in all that he can from a distance. Free to listen without spending energy engaging in conversation, the Observer absorbs details and inter-weaves possibilities and probabilities.

He protects the entire group by signaling when danger is imminent, quietly and thoughtfully alerting the leader without panicking the group.

Resourceful Expressions
- Focused and awake; patiently alert; silent until certain
- Curious, intuitive, insightful; reads signs
- Deeply present; wholistically observant
- Generalist, neutral; unattached to viewpoints or possibilities
- Possesses common sense; understands how people and things work
- Thorough in collecting data

Adaptations (Shadow)
- Asleep at the wheel; tuned-out; elsewhere; fails to show-up
- Cowardly; unwilling to bear bad news
- Secretive; reclusive
- Refuses to share knowledge that helps others
- Impatient; impulsive; jumpy
- Dramatic; Chicken Little; cries wolf

To reveal the light side of any situation

Optimist
(Dreamer, Polly-Anna, Utopian)

Optimist

Known as the upbeat one, the Optimist prefers the glass-half-full mentality. He will always be the one in the group to see the positive side of any situation, no matter how dire the problems and setbacks.

The Optimist unwittingly draws out criticism and negativity; the brighter the light of a sunny attitude, the deeper the shadow.

Resourceful Expressions
- Highly disciplined thinker; focused
- Joyous; sees the silverlining in everything
- Brings ideas and new possibilities to light
- Positive attitude; believes anything is possible
- Open-minded; curious; reaches higher
- Loveable, easy to connect with, life-affirming, motivational

Adaptations (Shadow)
- Stubborn in the face of criticism or doom-saying
- Impractical and unrealistic
- Prone to denial and fantasy; head in the clouds; airy-fairy
- Alienates pessimists and realists
- Exaggerates; stretches the truth to win support or make a point
- Uses positivity to mask pain; denies negative feelings and discomfort

To learn to fit-in and to model resourcefulness and independence

OUTSIDER
(Lone Wolf, Misfit, Orphan, Outcast)

Outsider

Known as the fifth wheel, the Outsider appears not to belong in the social group, family or organization. He is notoriously independent and wary of groups, wherever they gather. The Outsider also has keen radar for anyone in the crowd who is lost or unheard, often partnering or supporting them.

Through many years of fending for himself, the Outsider has acquired the survival skills for any environment.

Resourceful Expressions
- Self-motivated, independent; free agent
- Speaks for the underdog; empathic; caring
- Highly resourceful; skilled at doing for himself
- Mature beyond his years; old soul
- Willing to stand up for his own survival
- Unique; self-expressive; well-developed value system

Adaptations (Shadow)
- Stubbornly independent; loner; standoffish
- Rebellious toward leadership
- Refuses help when offered; plays the victim
- Hoards resources; secretive with natural gifts
- Lacks playfulness; tense and vigilant
- Defensive; ready for fight or flight
- Untrusting of life and other people

To ease conflict by creating harmony & resolution

PEACEMAKER

(Diplomat, Mediator, Passivist)

(Diplomat, Mediator, Passivist)

Peacemaker

Known as the dove, the Peacemaker exhibits a gentle and calm demeanor that puts others at ease. She is usually willing to put her own comfort and agenda aside for the greater good and group harmony.

Appearing as the objective witness, the Peacemaker is able to hear both sides of an argument, restore order and peace and bring resolution to bear on conflict.

Resourceful Expressions
- Highly empathic; understands compromise and win-win
- Good listener and calm communicator; easy-going
- Selfless; tuned to the greater good
- Values harmony, peace and getting along
- Easily engenders trust from others
- Open-hearted; relates easily to diverse personalities

Adaptations (Shadow)
- Passive; unwilling to act
- Refuses to take a stand; ambivalent about critical matters
- People-pleaser; tells others what they want to hear
- Lacks impartiality and objectivity; lacks boundaries with others
- Avoids conflict; surrenders too easily
- Betrays others; undermines those whose trust she has gained

To model grace, beauty and caring for others

PRINCESS
(Damsel, Helpless One)

Princess

Known as the beautiful one, the Princess performs an under-valued function in the world. While she appears to be helpless, she actually teaches others about compassion, refinement, grace and their own unique self-worth.

The Princess is able to soothe the battle-weary and dress the wounds of would-be leaders. She also rescues those in trouble or despair, while appearing to be the one in need of assistance.

Resourceful Expressions
- Appreciates refinement and beauty
- Loving, connective, heart-centered; other oriented
- Intuitive, patient, optimistic, hopeful
- Master at the soft skills and feminine arts
- Easily awakened to leadership and growth
- Vulnerable; unafraid of asking for help

Adaptations (Shadow)
- Selfish, self-centered; spoiled
- Prissy; fragile; unwilling to get dirty or work hard
- Condescending to those considered beneath her
- Childish; fantasy-driven; dreamer
- Impatient; impulsive; dramatic; impetuous
- Mesmerizes; charms others to get emotional needs met

To guard and protect the people, ideas or property ofothers

PROTECTOR
(Defender, Guardian, Knight)

Protector

Known as the knight in shining armor, the Protector takes personal responsibility for defending and protecting the honor or property of people and groups. She instinctively knows which argument or person is weakest and will step-up to temporarily align herself against the stronger opponent.

Others see the Protector as motivated by a kind heart, beneath a sometimes-gruff exterior.

Resourceful Expressions
- Strong debater and defender
- Keen observer of human motivation
- Responsible, courageous and kind
- Willing to put self in harm's way
- Trust her own instincts and intuition
- Gifted with physical or mental fortitude and strength

Adaptations (Shadow)
- Defensive and argumentative; self righteous
- Makes others wrong; exhibits black and white thinking
- Impulsive; fails to think through possible results of her action
- Lacks subtlety, diplomacy and grace
- Intimidates others with power and force
- Violently vengeful and competitive

To challenge the status quo through unconventional words and actions

PROVOCATEUR
(Mischief Maker, Underminer)

Provocateur

Known as a freethinking pioneer, the Provocateur's adventurous spirit sometimes gets the better of him. He can easily slip into the role of sneaky troublemaker. In these moments, he delights in the hormonal rush of inciting a pack mentality. Yet he also excels at challenges and often possesses experience, information and points-of-view that he selectively culls to persuade others. An ability to envision new possibilities from an old circumstance makes him a strong advocate for change.

A Provocateur causes dissension by challenging the status quo. He's an agitator. But he is also usually an intellectual, possessing a quick, razor-sharp wit. He habitually uses his formidable powers of provocation to offer alternative perspectives, freely challenging the belief systems of others. Provocateurs are quite common within roles that require debate, shocking their audiences with new or unconventional perspectives. Not surprisingly, they operate well within advertising and marketing, where their natural ability to intrigue and wedge images and ideas into the minds of others is highly valued.

Resourceful Expressions
- Observant; excellent problem-solver
- Provokes others to break free of their complacency or conformity
- Natural ability as a motivational speaker
- Calm under pressure

Adaptations (Shadow)
- Often amused by the discomfort of others
- Enjoys the sensation of shock value
- Boorish; relies on generalized stereotypes as a weapon
- Maintains the upper hand by stirring confusion among those around them

To say out loud what others are afraid to articulate

QUESTIONER
(Devil's Advocate, Pessimist, Skeptic)

Questioner

Known as the nitpicker, the Questioner finds the holes or gaps in ideas, plans and life in general. She gets a bad rap since her highest gift—to notice what isn't working or might be missing—is often experienced negatively by others.

But this analytically-minded individual's mission is essential: by sorting through the details of dreamed-up products, plans or ideas, the Questioner consistently sees opportunities for improvement and offers them up for consideration.

Resourceful Expressions
- Attentive to the details; discerning mind
- Highly analytical, focused, linear, logical, and systematic
- Proficient at de-bugging, fool-proofing and finding flaws in logic
- Able to imagine problems that others don't see
- Outspoken; not afraid to disagree
- Challenges ideas for the betterment of the project or goal

Adaptations (Shadow)
- Focuses intensely on what isn't working
- Does not generate or offer solutions
- Gets caught on the details; can't see the big picture
- Resists novel approaches or solutions
- Aggressive, negative and challenging communication style
- Attacks or ridicules those who disagree

To generate wealth and abundance through strategy and hard work

RAIN MAKER
(Midas, Miser)

Rain Maker

Known as the fortunate one, the Rainmaker attracts and creates abundance with ease. Through wisdom, strategy and more than a little luck, he repeatedly manifests wealth, freebies, upgrades and bonuses others only dream of. Yet his primary focus is often on maximizing his potential and personal expertise. The money or compensation he receives can be secondary.

Often envied by others, the Rainmaker is open to receive. But his gains are not charity or simply handed to him. A Rainmaker sets and tracks goals, with the specific intent to generate income. He has an innate ability to cultivate trustworthiness among others and frequently engages in social activities that allow him to network. Possessing a strong focus and sense of perseverance, he is a capable multitasker and more than willing to invest his energy into efforts that result in treasures both sought-after and unexpected.

Resourceful Expressions
- Optimistic; unrestrained by beliefs around money and other forms of compensation or reward
- Non-judgmental of self and others about financial matters
- Risk-taker; unattached to the outcome
- Strategic; identifies opportunities to create wealth in nearly every situation
- Philanthropist; fundraises or gives to causes outside of self

Adaptations (Shadow)
- Protective; withholds secrets to success
- Greedy, hoarder; fears losing wealth
- Blind to side effects of wealth accumulation
- Chooses wealth over family, friends, employees
- Money is used to increase status

To keep things grounded and in perspective

REALIST
(Pragmatist, Rationalist, Reasoner)

Realist

Known as the level-headed one, the Realist sees things for what they really are. Wary of hypothetical thinking and emotionality, she is extremely practical, checking the facts and keeping all things in accurate order and perspective.

The Realist values accuracy, efficiency, directness and orderliness and brings these qualities to everything she touches.

Resourceful Expressions
- Focused, goal-oriented and consistent
- Excellent observer; remains neutral
- Detached, unemotional, rational
- Has many general and practical hands-on skills
- Easily visualizes what works and what doesn't
- Views material reality as true and observable

Adaptations (Shadow)
- Obstinate, obstructive
- Critical; picky; overly focused on accuracy; perfectionistic
- Hypochondriac; complainer
- Kill-joy; overly scheduled and structured; not present
- Unable to work from the end or big picture; gets lost in details
- Challenges ideas based in creativity, imagination and fantasy

To model fearlessly trusting in one's own intuition

RISK TAKER
(Dare Devil, Thrill Seeker)

Risk Taker

Known as the high roller, the Risk Taker puts everything on the line to follow his own intuition. Others might see him as reckless and impulsive. What they fail to understand is the Risk Taker's strong inclination to tune-in his finely honed internal wisdom and exquisite perception.

Capable of deep self-trust the Risk Taker adventures far beyond where most care to risk.

Resourceful Expressions
- Highly perceptive, intuitive and self-knowledgeable
- Emotional intelligence valued more than intellect
- Willing to learn from mistakes; values trial and error
- Passionate about following an individualistic life path
- Comfortable with the unknown and the unpredictable
- Strong-willed; devoted to own ideas; self-trusting

Adaptations (Shadow)
- Reckless and impulsive; ignores intuitive hits
- Addicted to drama and excitement
- Self-destructive; workaholic; self-indulgent; addictive
- Harms self and others through needless repetitive trials
- Fails to engage rational thinking process when necessary to improve odds of success
- Trust issues; untrustworthy and untrusting of others

To model fearlessly trusting in one's own intuition

RULER

(Authority, Boss, Sovereign)

Ruler

Known as the one who steps forward to take control, the Ruler uses his authority and connections to affect change. He oversees the kingdom with care and wisdom, orienting his loyal subjects toward the direction he establishes. Political leaders and royalty throughout the world typically fit into this archetype. But it actually extends far beyond just the rare king, aristocrat, governor or global authority. A Ruler may inherit his "throne," through promotion or hire, serving as director of a company or non-profit organization.

A Ruler is always found at the top of every organized process or system, where he bears sole responsibility for the success or failure of the endeavor he oversees. It is not uncommon for this archetype to be focused on consolidating and maintaining his power and influence over others — often narrowing it until he alone is in control.

Resourceful Expressions
- Institutes policies and procedures that improve the standing of those under him
- Analytical; measures outcome before acting
- Big-picture thinker; responsible for the entire community
- Prevents chaos through control
- Self-confident, provides expert process knowledge
- Strong negotiator, mediates towards a desirable outcome

Adaptations (Shadow)
- Exerts power without counsel
- Constant fear of replacement; leads to authoritarianism
- Seduced by power and unquestioned authority; subject to corruption
- Shirks responsibility when things go awry, quickly blaming minions

To purify by cutting through illusion and artifice

SABOTEUR

(Bomber, Eradicator, Wrecker)

Saboteur

Known as the slate-cleaner, the Saboteur uses any means possible to wipe the slate clean, including humor, illness, aggression, chaos and accidents. He frightens others with his ability to uncover and annihilate the elephant in the room and his effect is seen most often when people and groups resist necessary change.

Often employing hidden or disguised agendas, coveted information, superb strategic skills and the element of surprise, the Saboteur can subtly undermine individuals or take down an entire process or group.

Resourceful Expressions
- Strategic; politically savvy
- Motives others toward positive change
- Truthful, honest, direct
- Spontaneous; adept at using the element of surprise
- Recognizes what isn't working
- Deep understanding of human motives and agendas
- Values purity and truth

Adaptations (Shadow)
- Reckless, explosive, destructive
- Aggressive or passive-aggressive
- Throws out the good with the bad when triggered
- Withholds or distorts vital information
- Manipulates through sneak-attacks and subtle power-plays
- Undermines others with gossip, hearsay and other tactics
- Unconscious, clumsy

To make sacrifices on behalf of a belief or cause

SACRIFICER

(Christ Figure, Martyr, Saint)

Sacrificer

Known as the one who "takes one for the team," the Sacrificer is willing to surrender every-thing to uphold his own cause or belief or the causes and beliefs of his group. Well known for acts of great courage, he often operates under a conscious or unconscious value system to which others have difficulty relating.

The true Sacrificer always acts according to his own conscience, regardless of personal consequences or recognition from others.

Resourceful Expressions
- Courageous; able to withstand criticism and disagreement
- Uncommonly strong values, beliefs and convictions
- Steadfast in the face of opposition and danger
- Willing to speak out to challenge the powers-that-be
- Self-effacing until tested or challenged
- Team oriented; fights for the good of the whole

Adaptations (Shadow)
- Prone to self-destructive behavior, sabotaging communication
- Stubbornly holds onto ideas and causes despite outcomes
- Uses guilt to manipulate; makes others uncomfortable
- Overly dramatic to make a point
- Threatens others to get his way
- Unconscious to self-sabotaging patterns and efforts gone awry

To hold and impart the wisdom of the ages

SAGE

(Crone, Guru, Master, Sensei, Wise Elder)

Sage

Known as the old soul, the Sage exudes the quiet wisdom of one who has learned life's deepest secrets. Unafraid to speak her mind, especially when members of the group are troubled or conflicted, the Sage reminds others to heed the lessons of the past.

To anyone with pure intention, she offers humankind's age-old wisdom while holding ideals of harmony and sanity for the future.

Resourceful Expressions
- Uses language, especially metaphor, intentionally; storyteller
- Calm stabilizing presence
- Teaches through example; role model; walks the talk
- Embodies the conscience and morality of the group, tribe or team
- Reminds others to let go when appropriate

Adaptations (Shadow)
- Out of sync with current thinking; proffers dated ideas
- Preachy, pedantic, long-winded, pompous
- Uses knowledge for his own aggrandizement
- Resistant to change, stuck in old ways and philosophy; anachronistic
- Controlling and manipulative
- Egotistical; manipulative; plays favorites

To use personal power to magentize desired objects

Seducer

(Charmer, Libertine, Siren)

Seducer

Known as the charismatic one, the Seducer possesses more tools in her arsenal than most. Her keen understanding of human nature–especially people's soft spots–allows her to display great power in magnetizing whatever she desires.

The Seducer can detach from others, compartmentalizing her feelings to achieve what she wants. She can be one's best ally or worst nightmare, depending entirely on her intention.

Resourceful Expressions
- Highly perceptive, intuitive and emotionally intelligent
- Skilled communicator and deep listener; engages others
- Goal-oriented and practical
- Extremely self-confident and self-aware
- Instinctive power-broker; intentional with personal power
- Good strategic planner

Adaptations (Shadow)
- Uses others for her own ends; emotionless and uncaring
- Sells out; trades on her own values; transactional
- Unconscious about her power and effect on others
- Self-destructive; low self-esteem
- Fails to stand on her own merits; enmeshes with others
- Takes self too seriously; gets caught in her own traps

To devotedly assist others or advance a cause

SERVANT

(Assistant, Helping Hand)

Servant

Known as the helpmate, the Servant is always available to assist those in need. She seems genuinely focused on others rather than on her own agenda. Kind, generous and open, the Servant's highest goal is to be in service, either to individuals, groups, or to the common ideal.

With her deeply held sense of devotion, the Servant's goodwill often extends far beyond most others' willingness to contribute and care.

Resourceful Expressions
- Kind, gentle, caring
- Highly resourceful and practical
- Generous and open to others; listens well
- Understands human nature; anticipates others' needs
- Cooperative team member
- Hardworking, tireless, devoted contributor

Adaptations (Shadow)
- Sacrifices own well-being; easily burns out; poor follow-through
- Gossips, meddles, gives unwanted advice
- Enables rather aids
- People-pleaser; doormat; tolerates poor treatment from others
- Needy; dependent; unable to get own needs met
- Unconscious agenda; wants something in return

To flexibly adapt to one's surroundings or situation

SHAPE SHIFTER
(Chameleon, Change Artist, Trickster)

Shape Shifter

Known as the one who reinvents himself, the Shape Shifter has many disguises and is often a natural mimic. Always the first to adapt to new surroundings, the Shape Shifter changes mannerisms, hair styles, names, personas, jobs, even friends and spouses, to suit his desired lifestyle or promote his current ideas.

The Shape Shifter is well received and loved by everyone he meets due to his natural capacity to be all things to all people.

Resourceful Expressions
- Highly adaptable and fluid
- Easily lets go of what's not working
- Perceptive and sensitive to her surroundings
- Abundantly creative, especially in communication
- Always presents a polished exterior, even during a crisis
- Empathic; reads energy and needs of others; responsive

Adaptations (Shadow)
- Truly knows no one, neither self nor others
- Flighty, volatile; Lacks staying power
- Avoids conflict and learning opportunities; escapist
- Shallow; flip; uncaring of others
- Unable to articulate values or stand on own merits
- Untrustworthy; lacks predictability; difficult to pin-down

To bring spiritual insight to the material human experience

SPIRITUALIST
(Medium, Mystic, New Ager, Prophet)

Spiritualist

Known as the "woo woo," the Spiritualist behaves as though connected to a completely different dimension. With eyes often closed or cast upward, the Spiritualist may appear more interested in the ethereal and the divine than in the people and objects inhabiting his everyday world. Motivated by higher ideals, the Spiritualist views everything from the largest perspective possible, often claiming cosmic insights unworthy of mere mortals.

Resourceful Expressions
- Right-brainer; accesses intuition and feeling; sensitive
- Brings lightness and high ideals to human processes
- Comes by wisdom easily; well-versed in deeper languages of life
- Easily changes modes; open to possibilities that few others can or will entertain
- Relates from a place of deep trust, calm, and respect

Adaptations (Shadow)
- Difficulty staying "down-to-earth;" flaky, spacy, un-grounded
- Relates better to divine than to human thinking
- Trouble being taken seriously; prone to quackery
- Claims higher knowledge than he actually possess; charlatan
- Hides in deep thought; connects to source for personal safety or gain; escapist
- Lacks practical experience of the world

To provide a grounding and stabilizing influence on others

STABILIZER

(Anchor, Father, Foundation, Support)

Stabilizer

Known as the rock, the Stabilizer is more felt than seen; he holds center when others are adrift. Happy to have a less glamorous profile than others, the Stabilizer is the one to whom others look to keep secure the values of a family or group.

The Stabilizer ensures that fundamental ideas, beliefs and values remain steady, consistent and unwavering. He anchors others so that all may reach solid footing.

Resourceful Expressions
- Stable, steady, practical, centered
- Instills sense of security by his presence
- Models diligence and self-discipline
- Prone to neither emotional highs nor lows
- Calm in a crisis; eschews drama and histrionics
- Returns chaos to balance and order

Adaptations (Shadow)
- Stubborn, stuck; slow to change
- Domineering, bossy, over-protective
- Workaholic, obsessive, plodding
- Expects too much of others; easily frustrated
- Unable to articulate feelings; avoids emotional matters
- Dismissive of risk-takers or seekers of change
- Controlling; unable to delegate; fears failure

To garner recognition for a performance

STAR

(Ace, Celebrity, Hotshot, Maven, Virtuoso)

Star

Known as the rock star, the Star represents the pinnacle of human endeavor. Because he is so adept at his craft, the Star's rise to fame is often swift, steep and meteoric.

These individuals shine their light so brightly that they often illuminate the room around them, commanding the attention and respect of all.

Resourceful Expressions
- Shows unusual gifts or virtuosity in a particular endeavor
- Brilliant mind; genius
- Unusual integration of body and mind
- Original; unique; singular
- Able to accomplish the nearly impossible
- Enlightens others simply by being oneself
- Big infectious personality; moves others energetically

Adaptations (Shadow)
- Suffers from loneliness and alienation
- Challenged to perform ordinary tasks
- Takes talent for granted
- Entitled, spoiled, childish; prima donna
- Defensive, underappreciated, misunderstood
- Burns out from over-effort
- Burns bridges rising to the top

To illuminate by sharing stories and metaphor

STORYTELLER

(Author, Bard, Narrator, Reporter, Speaker)

Story Teller

Known as the group historian, the Storyteller is the person who keeps and retells the myths and histories of society, connects with iconic figures, and relates with symbols of the ages.

Whether to entertain, teach, or pass on traditions, the Storyteller can burnish the bare facts until they have life and meaning. He leaves the judgment of truth or fiction to the ear of the listener.

Resourceful Expressions
- Excellent ear; listens and remembers well
- Unusual facility with language, speech and all narrative forms
- Keen observer of human behavior and universal patterns
- Comfortable in the realm of fantasy and make-believe; highly imaginative
- Finds new ways to connect people to the core of human experience
- Non-judgmental teacher, guide, and inspirer

Adaptations (Shadow)
- Can't distinguish truth from fiction; lives in fantasy
- Lies or tells half-truth to cover authentic feelings
- Prefers the life of the mind to real encounters
- Says too much; distorts reality to push personal agenda or beliefs
- Uses story to alienate or hurt others; twists tales toward own agenda or needs.
- Borrows or steals others' stories for own use; plagiarizes

To ensure self-preservation or the survival

SURVIVALIST
(Boy Scout, Extemist, Self-Reliant, Survivor)

Survivalist

Known as the "man with a plan B," the Survivalist is busy preparing for the end of the world or the worst-case scenario in any given situation. The Survivalist has provisions laid down and always knows the most expedient route out of the building or situation.

This guy is endlessly resourceful and will surprise others with his knowledge of esoteric facts and display of unusual practical skills, especially related to natural disaster. Just like the proverbial canary in the mineshaft, he is always alert for possible danger.

Resourceful Expressions
- Sensitive, alert, vigilant, observant, strategic
- Knowledgeable in core survival skills, emergency preparedness, and first aid
- Looks out for the health and safety of others
- Knows how to develop and execute a plan
- Exhibits a step-by-step, synthetic thinking style; practical
- Prepared to act on a moment's notice; ready

Adaptations (Shadow)
- Prone to paranoia, anxiety and panic
- Lets fear dominate thinking; paralyzed by what-ifs
- Saves himself first; cowardly
- Challenged by the here and now; too futuristic
- Pessimistic and helpless; nihilistic
- Hoarder; prone to scarcity thinking

To maintain the status quo or, better yet, return things to the way they used to be

TRADITIONALIST
(Conservative, Old Fashioned)

Traditionalist

Known as the one who is happy with the status quo, a Traditionalist longs for the comforts of certainty and stability. Slower to change, he strives to return to "the good old days" or a moment in time that embraced old-fashioned ideals. A Traditionalist who promotes values that coincide with healthier alternatives to modern living can enjoy quite a following. Traditionalists can be found among holistic health practices, environmental advocates, farm-to-table restaurants and markets, and shops that insist on artisan goods over cheaper, mass-produced substitutes.

In his perfect world, the Traditionalist has a stable job, reliable income and a healthy family. In exchange for these aspects of personal security, he is often extremely loyal to individuals and companies that help him achieve those goals.

Resourceful Expressions
- Boundless faith and optimism
- Values integrity; extremely loyal
- Responsible, trustworthy and diligent
- Strong attention to detail
- Decisive; guided by internal compass without lingering reflection
- Volunteerism; participates in social causes and service organizations

Adaptations (Shadow)
- Perceived as uninterested for adherence to innocent ideals
- Resists evolving technology
- Difficulty handling volatile people or relationships
- Submissive to hierarchy
- Dismissive of new ideas or anything that conflicts with conservative values

To sustain life by drawing upon the life force of others

VAMPIRE
(Extortioner, Freeloader, Leech, Sponge)

Vampire

Known as the "blood sucker," the Vampire relentlessly pursues sustenance by stealing the vitality of another. Often at the cost of other people's resources and well-being, the Vampire's mission is his own sustainability and longevity. While rarely seen as a resourceful archetype, he exemplifies devotion to personal survival, as well as the necessity to fight for one's own life.

Charismatic, seductive and even controlling, the Vampire charms his way through life, often gifting his victims by satisfying an unmet need. He fills his tank by lavishing attention on codependent victims willing to trade their energy simply to be seen, loved or adored — and sometimes those simply too timid to break free. The drain comes in moments when he turns passive-aggressive, using mind games to erode confidence and self-esteem. Eliciting sympathy for the latest in an inexhaustible list of troubles is another favorite tactic.

Resourceful Expressions
- Highly resourceful in meeting own needs
- Emotional intelligence provides insight into others
- Willing to help out with practical needs (but if done too often, this is used as leverage)

Adaptations (Shadow)
- Narcissist; only interested in end-game
- Negative, pessimistic attitude; endless complainer
- Emotionally dependent; unable to be alone or find entertainment outside the presence of others
- Hyper-critical; easily finds fault in others to nourish own need for superiority and control
- Draining to everyone around them; social circles tend to be extremely limited as a result

To protect boundaries from impact from others

VICTIM

(Inflicted, Scapegoat, Sufferer, Wounded)

Victim

Known as the "poor me," the Victim strongly identifies with those who have experienced injustice, violation and wounding. Grounded in compassion and awareness, the Victim engenders helpfulness in others, while healing himself and those around him.

But when unconscious, the Victim appears to be the one absorbing the impact of a negative situation or taking the fall for a glitch in the system. Attracting attention to his plight, however, often brings the awareness that helps himself and others transcend the negative.

Resourceful Expressions
- Easily empathizes with others, especially through shared experience
- Sets boundaries and alerts others to boundary violations
- Wounded healer; rescuer; helper; exhibits concern for others
- Elicits compassion in others; brings victimization to light
- Engenders helpfulness in others
- Believes in fighting for the cause

Adaptations (Shadow)
- Pessimistic; helpless; uncomfortable
- Drains, overwhelms and exhausts others; uses guilt to manipulate
- Self-centered, focused on own suffering
- Chronically dramatic; driven by negative emotion
- Needy; attention-seeking; demanding
- Gives up personal power for perceived protection
- Unconscious about own and others' motivations

To view endless possibilities from the highest vantage point

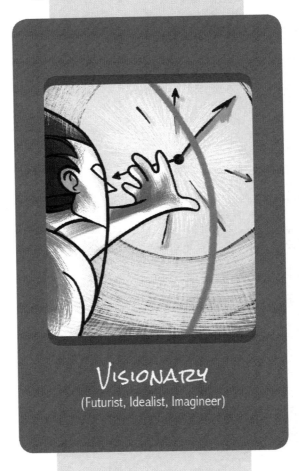

VISIONARY
(Futurist, Idealist, Imagineer)

Visionary

Known as the big picture person, the Visionary "dreams up" a variety of products, services, solutions or social ideas. He is the one at the table with the active imagination, constantly putting out something new for us to consider, often in an unfocused or non-linear way.

Frequently experienced as prolific storytellers, Visionaries speak in broad terms and sweep-ing ideals. They seem to be able to view the entire problem, challenge or situation from a higher vantage point.

Resourceful Expressions
- Highly imaginative, inventive and enthusiastic
- Easily brainstorms all possibilities
- Most comfortable with conceptual thinking
- Understands practical outcomes before they actually exist
- Inspires others; highly influential; motivator
- Focused on possibility and the positive in life

Adaptations (Shadow)
- Produces many and varied mental constructs with no mind for the details
- Channels ideas endlessly while rarely acting upon anything
- Thinks out loud; lacks focus and direction; challenged by linear thinking modes
- Easily overwhelmed by strength or number of possibilities
- Overwhelms others with excessive mental energy and large number of ideas
- Defensive; dismissive of criticism

To go forth and fight

WARRIOR

(Avenger, Knight, Samurai, Soldier)

Warrior

Known as the fearless one, the Warrior is perceived as fierce, brave and loyal. Oriented toward service, she pledges to defend and protect people, as she upholds ideals for the entire group.

Gifted with the discipline and strength of an athlete, the Warrior always keeps her eyes open for the advancement of the enemy. She remains watchful of those for which she cares the most.

Resourceful Expressions
- Courageous and tough minded
- Dedicated to others; trustworthy and reliable
- Fierce fighter; self-sacrifices for just causes
- Endures great hardship when necessary
- Avenger; seeks to right wrongs
- Values truth, justice, equity and equality

Adaptations (Shadow)
- Paranoid and argumentative
- Unnecessarily violent and aggressive
- Takes offense easily; looks for trouble; reactive
- Mercenary; easily bought; gun for hire
- Impulsive; acts before thinking; disregards consequences
- Uncouth; crude; out of touch with the gentler and kinder side of her nature

KOKORO MINDSTYLES®

To effect transformation using esoteric knowledge

WIZARD
(Alchemist, Magician, Scientist)

Wizard

Known as the "whiz kid," the Wizard is the person others see as capable of the impossible. Much of what the Wizard does is in some way "behind the scenes," or at least not visible by the average person.

Often the Wizard has gained his power through a series of challenges, wounds or secret acquisition of knowledge, sometimes spanning years of trial and error. He is often the lineage-holder of the esoteric knowledge of a group or tribe.

Resourceful Expressions
- Harnesses intellectual and material human power
- Possesses esoteric knowledge
- Effects change effortlessly
- Broad perspective spans past, present and future
- Understands both spiritual and physical laws of the universe
- Resourceful; concocts the perfect formula or situation

Adaptations (Shadow)
- Scattered, other-worldly
- Relates poorly to regular people; elitist
- Secretive; sneaky; elusive
- Refuses to share knowledge and techniques to help others
- Practices dark arts; sinister, evil; intention to harm
- Mysterious; misunderstood; actions evoke fear and mistrust
- Sells his technology to the highest bidder; corrupt

Made in the USA
Columbia, SC
01 August 2019